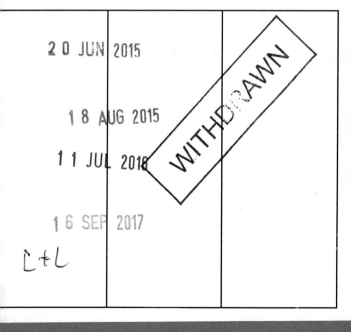

IT'S POLITICS . . . BUT NOT AS WE KNOW IT

IT'S POLITICS . . . BUT NOT AS WE KNOW IT

NICK FERRARI

LEADING BRITAIN'S CONVERSATION
DAB DIGITAL RADIO | 97.3 FM

First published 2015 by
Elliott and Thompson Limited
27 John Street
London WC1N 2BX
www.eandtbooks.com

ISBN: 978-1-78396-074-3

9 8 7 6 5 4 3 2 1

A catalogue record for this book is available from the
British Library.

Managing Editor, LBC: James Rea
Deputy Managing Editor, LBC: Tom Cheal

Typesetting: Marie Doherty
Printed in the UK by TJ International Ltd

global

Contents

Introduction

I can just picture it now: legions of political hopefuls stomping up and down the country, an eager look in their eyes, lips pursed at the ready ... Every five years we witness the same sorry spectacle. Mums of Britain, beware! In the build-up to a general election, an army of politicians will be queuing up to kiss your baby.

Don't let them do it.

I see this book as a kind of public health warning. When you get your 'Guide to Maternity' pamphlet from your GP, telling you why breast is best and that your child shouldn't sleep on its side, this book should be handed out alongside it.

When the nation's politicians pucker up to plant one on your beautiful baby, it's your duty as a citizen of this country to point a finger and laugh out loud ... and I'm going to tell you why.

Let's look at the state of politics today. We've got a load of MPs sitting in Westminster, in their own bubble, legislating for a population that they barely ever interact with. We've got the House of Lords, which is so out of touch it might as well be on the moon. The vast majority of those in Westminster are politics careerists who've come straight out of university and have never held down a proper job. Is it any wonder that people feel disconnected from all of this?

As the presenter of LBC's breakfast show, I get to talk to a fair few politicians. But I also get to talk to an awful lot of ordinary people; members of the public who phone in and tell us what they really think. This book is about the gap between the two — between the politicians on the one hand, and us, the people, on the other — and at the moment it's a mile wide.

There *are* some good guys out there, some good politicians doing fantastic work. All is not lost. But we need a change of culture and it's up to all of us to make it happen. It's about being real, being honest, and — most importantly, this is Britain after all — keeping a sense of humour.

Welcome to the new politics, Nick Ferrari-style.

1
The price of bread

Politics is serious. The way it is practised, and certainly the way it is presented by the majority of current politicians, is deadly serious. It's no laughing matter. But here's a funny story that sums up a lot about modern politics.

It was autumn 2013 and Boris Johnson, Mayor of London, had just appeared on *Newsnight* with Jeremy Paxman. This was at the height of party conference season, so all the guests wanted to talk about were nitty-gritty issues such as foreign policy, immigration, unemployment and God knows what else.

And this is a regular trick up journalists' sleeves — they also did it to George Bush Sr in the US presidential election — Paxman asked Boris Johnson the price of a pint of milk. Boris clearly doesn't buy his own milk because he fumbled it! He guessed 'about 80p or something like that', then tried to pretend he was talking about 'er, er, one of those biggish ones' when Paxman told him it was around 40p for a pint. Boris even tried to turn the tables, but Paxman was having none of it: 'I'm not standing for election, *you* are.'

So I had David Cameron on the show the following day and at the end I said something along the lines of, 'I have time for just one final question — the mayor was asked by Jeremy Paxman yesterday what a pint of milk costs,' and as I heard him chuckle down the line I said, 'I wouldn't do anything as low as that. Instead, Prime Minister, what's the cost of a value sliced white bread loaf at Tesco or Sainsbury's this morning? You'd know the price of that, wouldn't you, Prime Minister?'

Cameron said something like, 'Well, it's gonna cost you, er, well north of a pound, I mean, er, I actually don't buy the value sliced loaf, um, um, I've got a breadmaker at home which I delight in using and it turns out in all sorts of different ways but . . .'

After I told him the cost was 47p, he said something like: 'Look, I'm trying to get my children to eat er, er, the sort of granary — and they take it actually, they like my home-made bread.'

Then, 'A little plug for the flour made in my constituency — Cotswold Crunch — you get some of that, beautifully milled in the Cotswolds, you pop that in your breadmaker.'

And as he said this, I was thinking, 'Oh no, the *Daily Mirror*, they'll be googling "Cotswold Crunch" right now,' and, of course, they did and found out that it's handmade and it costs a whopping £30.20 for a 16kg sack.

He then went and asked if he could recommend a breadmaker to me.

And I said, 'Well actually, Prime Minister, I've tried them and the trouble with these breadmakers is that they take so long, they take about three hours . . .'

And he said, 'I'd recommend the Panasonic. There you are, that's another shameless plug. Very easy — even Nick Ferrari could work a Panasonic breadmaker.'

And I thought, 'God, the *Mirror* . . .'

Of course, they did google the Panasonic breadmaker — £139. Twice the weekly Jobseeker's Allowance! Totally out of touch.

There was loads of coverage the next day: 'The mayor doesn't know the price of a pint of milk!'; 'The PM doesn't know the price of a loaf!'

About a week later, I was at the *Daily Mirror* Pride of Britain awards and I saw the prime minister, so I proffered my hand and said, 'I'm terribly sorry, Prime Minister, about bread-gate the other day. Honestly, I had no idea . . .' He laughed and said, 'Oh, don't worry!' Then he reached down and picked up my bread roll, giving it a squeeze and joking, 'Can I just say, I don't think you got the texture of this one particularly right. You left the bread machine on too long, didn't you, Nick?' What he didn't realise was, it was Diane Abbott's bread roll — she was sitting next to me for dinner. To this day, Diane doesn't have a clue why the prime minister handled her bread roll!

Boris Johnson came in a couple of weeks after that and the issue was still bouncing around, it really was the gift that kept on giving. He sat down, and I could see that he was clutching a briefing piece of paper in his podgy paws and that it had nothing to do with Tube fares or the fight against crime, or his favourite topic of cyclists and cycle lanes — it listed the price of all sorts of items from baked beans to a pint.

We were live and I said, 'So, Boris, what are you going to do about the Hammersmith flyover? Shafting people in London, the state of the traffic jams and everyone with a job to get to . . .'

And he was waiting for me to say, 'Never mind that, I want you to tell me the price of a tin of Heinz Baked Beans!'

He waited so long that eventually he broke and said something like, 'Aren't you going to ask me the price of everyday groceries today?' Poor Boris, poised with his answers to crucial questions of the day like . . . how much is a tin of beans?

I said, 'No, I am not going to ask you that, but tell me, Mayor . . . do you happen to know the price of Fortnum & Mason champagne?' And, of course, he got it to within 50p!

Despite the silly outcome, this story makes a really important point. It's not about trying to catch politicians out for the sake of it. If they don't know the price of the basic foodstuffs that most people are surviving on, how can they claim to be our representatives?

It's crucial to be in touch, to live in the real world — whether you're a millionaire from the Bullingdon Club or you've worked your way up from the shop floor via the trade unions. Or even, as so many are these days, if you're coming straight into politics from the nursery via a degree in PPE (Philosophy, Politics and Economics, for the rest of us) at a proto-Westminster Oxbridge college with a name that you have to be born into landed gentry to know how to pronounce.

The majority in this country are working people living in the real world with all its demands, stretching their limited resources to get by the best they can, people who commute to their job every day, pay their bills and raise their families: they just don't recognise themselves, or their hopes and dreams, in our political leaders.

If you talk to people of my parents' generation — both of them actually served in the war; they were products of the 1920s — there was a real belief back then that politicians could make a difference. But now, people have very little faith in politicians: there is a worryingly low turnout at elections, and politicians just don't live like us any more. A lot of people participated in the Scottish referendum, which just goes to show that the electorate can be engaged when people really do care about the result. There will be a big fallout from the referendum result, and that needs to be addressed by our Westminster politicians — and they had better get it right.

Simply put, we need representatives who engage with us. The best way to make a connection with the electorate is to talk to us on our own terms. If you walk into a pub tonight and you find a group of our politicians sitting there, which one would you actually want to have a drink with, if they promised not to put it on expenses?

Could you bear to have a drink with Tony Blair? I very much doubt it.

Would you have a drink with Alex Salmond? Possibly, depending on your political views. Similarly, you might happily have a drink with Nigel Farage, who famously said 'every pub is a parliament'.

Would you enjoy a drink with Boris Johnson? I think so. Boris would just be a laugh. He's not going to use the opportunity to convince you about some political initiative; he would talk about something funny, he'd be normal.

Whenever Tony Blair tried to engage with people, it was pretty ugly. The distance between him and the public was huge — the distance between Boris, or Alex, and the public is about five inches.

I recall one time when Tony Blair was campaigning on the road and he bumped into a lady called Sharron Storer outside a hospital in Birmingham. Her partner had been admitted as a lymphatic cancer patient, and he'd had to be transferred to A&E because there were no beds in the bone-marrow transplant unit. This man, who was already extremely ill, was put at great risk of infection.

Ms Storer asked Mr Blair, 'What are you going to do? ... He suffered terribly. Would you like to tell me how you are going to provide these people with better facilities? ... All you do is walk around and make yourself known but you don't do anything to help anybody.' She said, 'All he kept saying was, "They're going to do better, they are trying." But he has been trying for years, in my opinion, and they still haven't got it right.'

Tony Blair was trying to shift the responsibility onto hospital staff rather than admit that the health-care system was failing because of his policies. As the then Conservative Party Chairman Michael Ancram said at the time, 'This afternoon in Birmingham, four years of Labour spin were crushed by four minutes of reality.'

Our leaders need to understand that there are no shortcuts to building a relationship with the electorate. We will not be fobbed off with toothy smiles and empty promises. Only when they really understand the pressures of real life outside Westminster, will they be able to grasp the issues that matter to us and respond by pushing those concerns to the top of the political agenda.

2
The political disconnect

Politicians cannot hope to bridge the gap between their ideas and our world if they have never held a proper job outside the political arena. It's just not the same for them as it is for us, and there's no substitution: MPs need to work. So many graduates emerge from their hothouse degrees in PPE at Oxford or Cambridge, carry a bag for an MP for a few months while they're supported by the bank of mum and dad and, the next thing you know, they're on their way to being one themselves.

If you've worked in another industry or some sort of trade, it gives you knowledge and a skill-set. It doesn't matter whether you're selling cornflakes, driving taxis, or working in a hotel; you will have developed some skills and insights about all sorts of things that would benefit you if you were ever tempted to join the political fray.

I'd like to see a rule come in whereby politicians are obliged to go out and work in industry for a couple of years before they take high office. It's their duty to show that they can run something in the real world and that they understand the responsibilities that ordinary people undertake.

The chancellor of the exchequer ideally needs to have run a corner shop. They need to have had the morning papers out by seven o'clock and the milk delivered by six-thirty. After that, they will realise just how hard it is for us to earn the money that they like to spend. For too long they've thought that money appears simply by making a phone call and stating, 'I'd like to build a battleship.' The reality is that commoners like us have to slave our nuts off to pay our taxes so that they can build these battleships.

After working at real jobs, our leaders should begin to realise that, in order to represent us, they need to know their remits inside-out. We, the public, can tell whether they are on a mission to improve our lives or whether they are motivated by freewheeling ambition.

What we have at present are too many career politicians with no worldly experience, clawing their way through office after office. In fact, we have too many MPs altogether — there are 650 of them, as opposed to 535 Members of Congress for the entire United States of America!

Under the Labour government, we got through so many home secretaries that it was easier just to give them numbers than remember their names: 'Farewell, number three, and come in, number four'; 'Ah, I see number seven has gone, bring on number eight.' There was no time to get attached to them. Their posts seemed like a means to an end, just a step on a ladder.

In the Nick Ferrari Cabinet, if you were made secretary of state for Education, unless you were found fiddling your expenses or you were an al-Qaeda terrorist, you would stay with Education, because you would have invested a great deal of time in learning everything about it, and you would demonstrate an abiding love and passion for it.

A quick turnaround doesn't make sense. We need one politician in one office so that they come to be experts in their field and they can accumulate experience to do the job properly. The way ministers are allocated these days is like taking a publisher and suddenly putting them in charge of milk production, or Northern Ireland, when they don't know the first thing about it.

In political situations regarding compli- cated and volatile issues that affect every aspect of our families' lives, would you rather trust a twenty-five-year-old policy wonk or someone who has successfully run a business, who might actually know something about how the world works?

Part of the appeal of Nigel Farage is that he has done a proper job. You may like him or loathe him — and many of us are still undecided — but you have to hand it to him: he was a successful stockbroker, he made a lot of money and he's got a big house in Kent. I admire that.

Look at Sajid Javid, MP for Bromsgrove. At the time of writing he's the Conservative

Secretary of State for Culture, Media and Sport. He's possibly the future of the Conservative party, if you ask me.

The son of an immigrant, his father was a Pakistani bus driver and he attended state schools before being the first in his family to go to university, to study politics and economics. A former investment banker, he now has an impressive personal fortune. He sends his children to private school and doesn't make a secret of it: he does what he thinks is best. He calls it exactly the way he sees it, without slavishly following traditional party lines, and people like that. As long as he stays true, I think he is the sort of person who can break through the political mould.

Two other rising stars, for Conservatives and Labour respectively, are Esther McVey and Gloria de Piero; McVey is currently MP for Wirral West and Minister of State for Employment, and de Piero is MP for Ashfield and Shadow Minister for Women and Equalities. Both have been television presenters and they've worked in several jobs as journalists, as well as in other business areas. They will have been exposed to people at the best of times and the worst of times as that's what happens in journalism, particularly when you're on a local paper: you have to interview the widow who's just discovered that her husband's been killed in a hideous crane accident. But you also see the great times, such as when a wonderful old couple are celebrating fifty happy years of marriage, or a family's blind dog on wheels has a litter of fifteen healthy puppies.

Parliament is an insular world and the public perception of this is not helped by the MPs themselves. It was reported recently that the Independent Parliamentary Standards Authority recommended an 11 per cent pay increase for MPs, which is wrong when MPs are preaching austerity to everybody else. They're holding pay, they're letting people go, firing people, restricting overtime, so why do they deserve a rise where ordinary hardworking people do not?

Over the years, many MPs have maintained

that the price of alcohol should not be raised in the House of Commons bars; bars that are subsidised by UK taxpayers who are riven by the 'cost of living crisis', as politicians themselves like to call it. Obviously, MPs work at the House of Commons, in too many instances they probably sleep with people who also work there, and they drink £1.4m of booze there — well, wouldn't you, if you could buy a pint at about half the usual price in London?

This is galling for the man who does a heavy physical job and wants a pint at the end of the day, who has to cough up nearly a fiver for it, while these Westminster guys, with salaries over seventy grand, are getting theirs on the cheap at the taxpayer's expense. It's hardly an essential spend now, is it?

I don't know if you've ever been to the House of Commons, or to Millbank, but I have, and I can tell you that politicians' sense of their own importance is absolutely all-consuming. The party conferences are a good illustration of this breathtaking insularity. I've attended a few of these over the years, but I'll only go for one day. I can't get out of there quickly enough, because there is no conversation outside of what they're all up to.

Perhaps you work in an office or a factory or maybe you drive a bus, and when you get in the canteen or you meet colleagues at the water cooler, you talk a little bit about what's happening at work and your workmates: you know, 'Warren lost the account' or 'Sophie's been promoted' or 'Reg was caught banging the managing director', but you don't talk about it ceaselessly. They do. There's nothing else on their radar and there's no one saying to them, 'Listen, there's a world out there and what you just said is actually not that important. Nobody cares.' They have too many people telling them how great they are.

Tell it like it is

The flip side of the 'bread-gate' story is that politicians are so out of touch that they feel like they can't say things that the rest of us would say. What I've learned from my callers is that what people really want is honesty. People talk about mixed messages, and that's often when my callers become confused and get quite angry. I don't know why politicians do it, but too many times, when they're asked a question, they can't give a definitive answer either way. They're too frightened to say it, or they don't know.

There was a big row about paying trades-men in cash. Cameron was asked, 'Do you ever pay tradesmen in cash?' and he said he had done, but never to avoid tax, and didn't really answer properly. They asked Boris Johnson and he said, 'Of course I have, and it's up to them to pay their taxes.' And he's right! If you pay your window cleaner twenty pounds in cash, what he or she chooses to do with it is nothing to do with you. This example shows just how paranoid these people get. It's absurd. It's not up to me to ask my cleaner how she conducts her affairs, and most people would say the same. But almost everyone working in politics seems to feel that they can't be honest with us.

If our politicians fessed up to the truth, they might win our respect. At a mayoral debate this year, we got on to cycling. Boris was talking about how much he loved cycling and he didn't want cyclists in London to wear tabards with a number on the back: there is a perception that, in London and I'm sure in other cities in Britain, cyclists sometimes cause the accidents in which they're injured or even killed, because some of them don't respect traffic lights and try to nip in on the inside of bloody great juggernauts, where the drivers can't see them.

So in some instances — certainly not all — cyclists are regarded by other road users as being their own worst enemy. The idea behind the tabards is that if you're cycling like an idiot and I've got you on camera, I can track you down and point out the terrible risks you are taking, and perhaps you'll be fined, or sent on a cycling awareness course.

Boris made a comment along the lines of, 'I don't believe in it, I think it takes away the freedom and it takes away the fun. The great joy of cycling is that you just say, "Oh, it's a beautiful day, I'm going to cycle by the river," and off you go.' He continued: 'One of my great recollections is when my children were younger, I once cycled with one of my children on the handlebars, and one of my children holding on to me behind.'

Of course I had to ask, 'Well, how safe was that?'

And Boris replied, 'It's not safe.'

'So why did you do it?'

He paused and said, 'I did it because it was fun.'

Well, you should have heard the cheer he got from the audience. They were thinking, 'Oh, how fantastic that someone is just being honest!'

When I was younger, and much, much lighter, I was also carried on the handlebars of my brother's bicycle, because that's what you did. But nowadays you'd have an army of these health-and-safety people coming down on you, or even social services coming round to ask you what you think you're doing!

That's why it was so refreshing to hear a politician being real, being honest: not just toeing the party line — or the PC line.

Political correctness

In my view, political correctness is a bit like 'the public interest', or the G spot: it's impossible to define and very difficult to find. Sometimes I get a sense of what it is. Fortunately, callers on radio shows like mine have now stopped saying, 'It's political correctness gone mad.' Even newspaper columnists seem to have stopped.

I think most of us will agree that some actions in the name of political correctness can go very wrong. In many cases, there was never a problem in the first place. Take the idea of Wintervals, those public events that were first held in Birmingham to encourage non-Christians to celebrate the Christmas season — what a load of old cobblers. Many hardworking Muslims run corner shops, selling Christmas decorations and wrapping paper and the 'last-minute booze because Auntie's coming round so you need to run to the shop to buy a bottle of Bell's'.

These guys are commercial traders and, on the whole, they don't give a monkey's about political correctness, or being given preferential representation over the traditions of the country they're living in. On the contrary, they're quite happy about Christmas because it's a chance to make extra money and the punters are in a generous mood.

For the group of mad white liberals — with a small 'l' — who fret and insist, 'But we must be inclusive!' I think it starts to get quite dangerous. Christianity is and should be the dominant faith in this country. Of course you can do all your Hanukkahs and Eids and Diwalis and that's great; we enjoy learning about it and sampling your culture's delicacies. But it is madness to call it wrong that, as we are a Christian country, we will put on a nativity play.

Politicians are very happy to lecture us on just about everything. Under the Labour government there was a suggestion that every new bath should be fitted with a special sort of thermostat to limit the temperature of our bathwater. Look, if I want to run my bath so hot that I get a red sock when I put my foot in it, why should anybody stop me? I believe in a country where these kinds of private matters are my decision.

Greater individual responsibility is common sense. It's also a principle that extends to politicians who need, when they believe it is in the public interest, to think independently and to challenge party orthodoxies.

Show some backbone

It's wrong that good politicians, such as Jacob Rees-Mogg, are excluded from high office for not toeing the party line. In business, a good chairman seeks people's views, but politics is all too often just about agreeing with the leader, and career advancement. Few politicians follow their own conscience. Boris is doing a good job because he's his own man.

For similar reasons, I genuinely admire a Canadian Liberal politician called Jean Chrétien, who was prime minister there for more than a decade. When he took power, immigration needed to be addressed and they'd overspent. Similar, you could argue, to what has been happening here in the UK. Chrétien resolved to fix things. In effect, he said, 'Of course I'm going to keep the army going and keep the lights on, but that's not all that matters.' He saw out many demonstrations, people screamed abuse at him, yet he kept his mind focused on the job he had set out to do and stuck to his principles. He risked being unpopular, like Margaret Thatcher in her early years as prime minister, and was, in fact, re-elected.

In the UK, I greatly admire Zac Goldsmith. He's the Conservative MP for Richmond Park.

It probably helps that he's richer than Croesus and better-looking than Jude Law, but he's a very smart, well-educated and ambitious man. As part of the Eton set, he could have effortlessly sailed into the Cabinet, where he would not have been out of place at all — they could all have talked about the great days of roasting fags in front of the fire, and goodness knows what else.

But Zac has stayed utterly true to his constituents. The big deal in his area has been the proposed third runway at Heathrow. You can imagine the level of opposition out there — those poor souls have suffered enough, they probably never get any sleep — and Goldsmith made it clear that if his party dropped opposition to the extra runway he would resign immediately and force a by-election.

Now, Cameron could really have done with him toeing the party line, which is: keep your gob shut, wait for what's in the Davies Report to come out, fall into line, vote and get on with the rest of our lives.

But Zac won't play any Tory games, so that, under Cameron, he will probably never get an advance within the party. He'll never be an undersecretary, minister of state, and then something in the Cabinet. And he doesn't care. He's a young man, in his forties, acting with real conviction. The Tories would really miss him. Politicians like that, who are true to their constituents, we should absolutely treasure. They're too few and far between.

Looking on the other side of the fence, there's Kate Hoey, Labour's former Minister for Sport and the Labour MP for Vauxhall, who vigorously opposed the war in Iraq, almost from day one. She kissed goodbye to a Cabinet position within the Labour government at that time, simply because she felt it was wrong and it didn't represent the interests of her country.

Very, very brave.

These people won't settle for what they believe is wrong, even though they're all ambitious folk and must be pretty bonkers to have gone into politics in the first place. But they say, 'That's it, you've crossed a line. I'm going to drive into a career cul-de-sac, because I stand for what my constituents want. I refuse to compromise my principles and vote as whipped.'

That doesn't mean doggedly sticking to something once you know it's wrong. Vince Cable, for example, started in the Labour Party, before moving to the Lib Dems. Doesn't the fact that he can admit he has changed his mind make him a man of principle?

There's an idea that the young are all socialists. Churchill is reported to have once said: 'Show me a young Conservative and I'll show you someone with no heart. Show me an old Liberal and I'll show you someone with no brain.' Our opinions evolve throughout our lives — we change partners, jobs and houses. If you are persuaded by another point of view, I think that's positively to be encouraged. But you do have to develop your own convictions: it's not like deciding 'I fancy wearing this hat today.'

The ability to hold a conviction and to speak

of it truthfully and honestly is something to be greatly admired in a politician — though it is a rare trait. One of the people I've been most impressed by was Mo Mowlam. My callers and I were all ready for her when she came on the show — they were furious that she had broken bread with the IRA, people who had bombed the army, members of the royal family and ordinary citizens. They wanted to know why she had sat down with these people.

Mo responded with one of the most open and rational explanations I've heard from a politician. It came from the heart. She said to this caller something like, 'You have to know it was very, very difficult for me. I've visited barracks where soldiers had been killed, blown up. I've sat down with commanding officers, I've sat with mourning wives and mums. But the business of politics sometimes requires that you sit down with the enemies you despise. You have to look them in the eye and you just have to try to make peace and you have to be bigger than the events that precede it.'

I think she was absolutely right. It's a very difficult thing to do, but she was a very brave politician — and an honest one.

It's all about image

We've lost many of the real characters in politics, because they all have to be so careful nowadays.

Public relations executives manage everything. PR, being concerned with appearance and with media-friendly soundbites, can prevent politicians from advancing tough-but-true policies and arguments. It's often the case that if you try to please everyone, you end up pleasing no one.

I blame Robin Day. He set a benchmark in political style. Of the great figures of the past, Lloyd George, Churchill and, certainly, Harold Wilson would never have become leaders today. They might have been great politicians, but they didn't have this look, this somewhat incredible, slick, presidential feel that our politicians often strive for now.

Don't get me wrong, politicians have been conscious of their image for as long as they've existed. The Romans declaimed their rousing speeches with memorable phrases and Julius Caesar's crown of laurels, that hid his baldness, became a brand, so much so that we all instantly recognise him well over two thousand years later.

Churchill harnessed that same old Roman rhetoric power when he gave his famous speeches. Everyone pictures him smoking his cigar; it was a great prop. But whether you're wearing a donkey jacket or a tweed one, make-up or not, the public immediately see through you if you're trying too hard and there's nothing behind it.

It's like dads dancing. When they get it right, it's so good that you don't realise it until afterwards. It's when they get it laboriously wrong that you can't bear it. Disraeli wore long ringlets and frilly shirts and he created a brilliantly recognisable image for himself, but take William Hague and his baseball cap — it's just grotesque. A political nerd like Hague will never look streetwise by perching a baseball cap on his pate. The truth is, we need more ugly politicians, which is why I could possibly be prime minister. We'd have a Cabinet of ugly people. Nick Clegg's not a bad-looking bloke, but George Osborne had his hair done and it looks pretty frightening — like Action Man gone wrong. I think he could do with going to see Nicky Clarke; maybe I can put a call in for him but, in the meantime, he could stay in my cabinet.

But, more seriously, it's when politicians try to fake their genuineness — when they try to connect, and it's not real — that's where they really go wrong.

When Gordon Brown was prime minister, he decided to broadcast a video about the expenses scandal from beside the marble fireplace at Number 10. He'd clearly been told to try and be animated, to gesticulate and, worst of all, to smile. But it was a fake smile — not only could we all see straight through it but, boy, it would frighten the horses! It looked just like the evil smile of a Bond villain. He looked bloodless. As you watched him, you couldn't help but wonder, 'What does he know that we don't, to make him smile like that? He's obviously got my mother hostage round the back.' You can just hear the PR team saying, 'Whatever happens, Gordon, try to look normal.'

Gordon Brown was perceived as being a remote and unapproachable prime minister, so he was obviously encouraged to listen to a team of image-makers who would train him to appear to be 'a man of the people'. He would have been better off conducting his fireside speech in his usual dour manner, like a judge reporting that he had punished the criminals and that moral order had been restored. The truth is that his message was eclipsed by the phoney persona he'd been advised to adopt.

The separation of politicians from real life means that, when they reach a certain level, they over-rely on special advisors and directors of communication. If you get the wrong one, or the wrong team, you can make terrible mistakes. Here's an example.

As part of the 2014 World Cup fever, every home in the land got a copy of the *Sun*, and there were pictures of Cleggy holding up a *Sun*, David Cameron holding up a *Sun*, and then there's Ed Miliband holding up a *Sun*.

What made it seem like a good idea, when the request came in, 'Would Mr Miliband please pose for a picture with the special promotional *Sun*?', to say yes? I wasn't working on it at the time, but I did work on the *Sun* for many years and I do know people who work there. In Liverpool, you might as well say you've got triple herpes as say that you read the *Sun*. To be seen to support that paper — well, there's nothing worse. You'd probably get struck from the family bible.

Miliband didn't realise. He went to Liverpool, the absolute heartland of the Labour vote, and understandably the local media — the *Post* and *Echo*, the local radio stations — went absolutely nuts. So the next thing was that he had to say that perhaps it was a mistake and he shouldn't have done it. And, brilliantly, the day after that, the *Sun* attacked him for not sticking to his principles.

So in the space of just three days he endorsed a product, which he then realised was an idiotic thing to do, and then the very people who put him onto it turned on him as well. Ed probably thought he was onto a good PR stunt but he and his advisors weren't thinking about his core supporters — the people who really count — and it backfired on him.

He isn't the only one, though. Remember David Cameron's horribly staged photo, watching the Olympics with a remote control in his hand? Or Tony Blair's unfortunate 'claim' that he'd seen Jackie Milburn play at Newcastle United, which was just impossible because he wasn't playing at that time (he was later found to have been misquoted, but the damage was done)?

It just looks desperate.

Politicians visit our schools, offices and factories, often wearing suits and ties, thus placing an immediate distance between them and the people who work there. There's the shot of Ed Balls and Andy Burnham at a children's playground in Brixton. There's a swing rope going across the sand pit and these two grown men are hanging out with the kids, in their white shirts and ties, swinging.

You can see the shock on the children's faces. These poor kids were being told, 'By the way, children, you must behave because this man could be chancellor of the exchequer and this man could be leader of the party'. No wonder they're not going to vote. The kids are thinking, 'They won't even let me play in the sandpit.' Something very like this playground scene ended up in the political comedy *The Thick of It*, and it's no wonder.

Some people might say that these details of politicians' images are trivial — merely surface stuff. But if you look at Ed Miliband's 'bacon-sarnie-gate', you can see that this trivia is of a different kind: it actually resonates with people as significant that he can't eat a bacon sandwich in a normal way, because it shows that he's just not like us.

When politicians get it right, it's wonderful . . . I'm thinking of Ann Widdecombe. Her dancing on *Strictly Come Dancing* was fantastic. She actually got through to the quarter-finals of *Strictly*! It's great entertainment because she's got a sense of humour about herself. She knows she's not like the people who usually win these shows: she's not slim with long legs and blessed with a fantastic body shape and she knows it. That's why I think I love her. I would like to partner Ann Widdecombe at dancing; it would be sensational. Don't think there wouldn't be a little bit of dirty dancing; there'd definitely be a bit of twerking. 'Is it twerking for you, Ann?'

When politicians try to mould their images to seem approachable, people can just see through it. All politicians will craft their image to a certain extent, even if it's a kind of anti-image, but the important thing is to craft it in such a way that it isn't at odds with your own personality, and to make sure that it actually appeals to people rather than separating them from the masses they're there to represent.

These days, when PR teams and media experts get involved, the resulting speeches and presentations seem so glib. We had such good soundbites in the past, truly unforgettable ones such as Thatcher's 'The lady's not for turning'. But now we have horrible empty ones, such as 'Winning over hearts and minds', which was big in 2012. 'We're Britain, we're better than this'. What does that mean? People see through them. 'The Big Society', what's that all about? Nonsense. I'll bet you Cameron doesn't know either. Sold to him, probably by some American guru he bought in. Not a bloody clue.

In 2011, Ed Miliband was filmed on television answering a variety of questions about teacher strikes in almost exactly the same, quite lengthy, way. Seven times in nearly identical fashion, like a robot. 'These strikes are wrong when negotiations are still going on. Parents have been let down because the government has acted in a reckless and provocative manner. Both sides should get around the negotiating table and put aside the rhetoric to stop this kind of thing happening again . . . ' And again. And again. You could almost see the cogs whirring and white smoke and tiny springs popping out from behind his ears.

There's a great guy, Lieutenant Colonel Tim Collins, an ex-army officer of the Irish Guards. You may recall a speech he made when we were going into Iraq in 2003. It sounded and felt like prosaic Latin. He said, and I paraphrase, 'We're going into the cradle of civilisation, you must treat everybody with respect, if you fall we will be there for you, you will not be left.' It was truly stirring stuff; it was Churchill-esque. That man actually toyed with the idea of being a police commissioner, before he realised that it was all bogus rubbish. The last thing we need are puppets whose anonymous string-pullers only care about quick-fire media hits. We need someone like Tim Collins to be in charge; someone who can speak directly from the heart, inspire people to work through the hard times, and deliver the goods.

With so many politicians, it's as though they've been coded for the programme in 'Lessons need to be learned: Part 3'. You know, 'Lessons need to be learned from this tragedy, and we're going to hold a robust debate about this . . .' You're never going to hear this from Farage, you're never going to hear it from Boris. They simply don't deal in robot-speak. We're sick of hearing that there are 'lessons to be learned' for the health service, the police force and everybody else. Dear God, how many lessons are there? Endless, and I've had enough.

I think there's an increasing American-isation of what we do here, because we look across to their presidential debates. And, as a result, we're dangerously close to letting style matter more than substance. Look back at the video of Tony Blair when he first walked into Downing Street as prime minister in 1997. Goodness me, he's a young man. He looks fantastic; he's got a young wife and a young family. It's all great. Everybody feels fantastic, and isn't it just bloody marvellous?

But when you put so much onus on the slick presentation, you can lose touch with reality. If you have a hard time being honest with the electorate, you're lost just when you need them most.

We need to accept that politicians are human, and they can't get it right all the time. We all make mistakes. But how many of them know how to say sorry? I don't think Gordon Brown even knows the word. Did he ever offer regret for anything that he did? Look at the Chilcot Report, the Iraq inquiry Brown announced in 2009 — it didn't come until some seven years after that war broke out. It's a scandal.

Of course it's wrong that Saddam Hussein apparently dropped people who opposed him into shredding machines and that he gassed his own people. But if that was the reason we went into Iraq — if it was about regime change — they should have been honest. Instead, the government pretended that it was all about weapons of mass destruction and whether they could drop a bomb in Basingstoke. It was all a load of cobblers — we know that now.

Yet we still have Tony Blair saying what a great job he did. He's totally out of step with the people. We don't want to see these PR-managed politicians any more. We want to see a real effort to get to the issue; genuine conscience where it counts. We need candour. We can tell when something resonates as true.

A two-way dialogue

The key to engaging is to really connect with the public — to care, to talk, and to listen. There are no shortcuts. What politicians need to under-stand — and some of them are maybe beginning to see this — is that they can no longer simply talk to us, that we need to speak back, and it really is a dialogue. Up until a few years ago, it was a monologue. They would tell us what to do, we'd bump into each other every five years at the polls, it would normally go badly, and then that would be over. Now they realise they need to take into account the needs, feelings, desires and wishes of the electorate.

I have huge respect for Ken Livingstone, and he is now my colleague at LBC, but we got off to rather a bad start. When the Iraq war was coming to an end, I had suggested that we should have some sort of parade to celebrate the soldiers' return, as we did after the Falklands, as a gesture of thanks to the men and women who'd put their lives on the line. All we needed was Ken's permission, as Mayor of London. Initially he refused, then he proceeded to ignore our calls to discuss it further, which I thought was just plain rude. After trying unsuccessfully for four days to get a response, I told his office I would put the phone number on air if I didn't hear back. They obviously thought I wouldn't do it.

I went on air the next day: 'You know, I've been trying to get you a response from the mayor at City Hall since Tuesday, to hear whether he thinks a homecoming parade is a good idea. Look, I'm terribly sorry, this is going to cost you a few pennies, but if just a couple of you could ring the following number, that will get you straight through to the mayor's office, and if you could just say, "I'm ringing on behalf of Nick Ferrari — is there any chance that you could support the idea of a homecoming parade?"'

It took the switchboard down. City Hall went crazy; they obviously had to change the phone number. Ken wrote to my employer saying I should be fired, he wrote to my agent saying I should be fired, I think he might even have written to my mum.

Of course, in hindsight, he was completely right and it would have been hideous. Luckily, although the experience did colour the relationship for a while, everything is fine now. I respect him because he got it right, and I like to think that in a way he respects me because, although he was beyond furious at the time, decent politicians often quite like people who have that streak of anarchy, who take the attitude, 'Come on, we pay for you lot, answer the questions.' He should have done. Politicians are learning to ignore us at their peril, because we can air our grievances in an instant.

The reason why a station like LBC is doing so well in its political coverage is that the traditional form of politics, with people going round and banging on doors, doesn't work any more. The game has moved on. We all know that like-minded groups can form demonstrations alarmingly quickly.

When the young soldier Lee Rigby was killed near Woolwich barracks in 2013, the police services should have realised sooner than they did that the story was running on Twitter and that the men were being named there at the same time as the official line was being released as 'two men have been arrested in connection with . . .' and revealing nothing else. Traditional media, i.e. radio, television and newspapers, have to play catch-up with new social media platforms.

We've seen the political effect of hashtags on Twitter; it can be a real call to arms. It's another way for people to rally together and get their voices heard. Politicians are now tweeting all the time as well — they realise that social media is very important, even if they often get it wrong.

Ed Balls famously tweeted his own name, just 'Ed Balls', in 2011. Presumably he was googling himself and opened the wrong application — rather embarrassing. Now he makes an anniversary of it every 28 April — he's turned it to his advantage and it's quite funny.

Occasionally you get an idiot who's a bit drunk and says something offensive or just completely misjudges the mood.

Twitter reaches a wide audience very effectively, but it's conversation that really moves things along. What people like Clegg, Boris and even Nigel Farage are trying to do on LBC, with the phone-ins that are open to the public, is very laudable.

The idea originally came from New York,

where the mayor holds a phone-in fairly regularly. LBC aims to emulate this by encouraging our own senior politicians to participate in its programmes. Tony Benn was the first to agree, saying, 'Yes, I will come in but I have two requirements. I like strong tea served continuously, and I like to puff on my pipe.'

The tea was no problem, but the smoke detectors in the office went off if anybody so much as lit a match, leading to the whole building being shut down. After long conversations with management and the guys in health and safety, and hours spent looking at smoke detectors, finally it was agreed that, yes, they could be disabled just this once. So in came Tony Benn, and we were all very excited.

Tony certainly liked a lot of tea, but he was attached to his pipe to an incredible degree. I have, on occasion, had tears in my eyes during emotional points of my shows, but never just because of tobacco. And this even though my father had been a regular pipe-smoker, so I grew up with it. But Tony Benn created an impenetrable fug that probably took years off my life. The next time he came on the show, I said firmly that we would be doing it at a different studio — with a window and a fan.

In our smoke-free studio, I've been lucky enough to have conversations with Clegg after the show and he's always fascinated to hear about the issues that have been discussed on the other four days. I think there is a new breed of politician who realises that this exchange with the public is the future of politics. If you ask Nick Clegg why he decided to do the 'Call Clegg' phone-in slot, he answers it was to get over the heads of all the Westminster journalists. And what's fascinating is that Nick would sometimes, as he was picking up the headset, ask, 'I wonder if we're going to get a lot of calls about X?' But what appears to be a huge issue in Westminster and, I have to say, the media as well, often doesn't play out at all for the public. There's a lot to learn.

People care about issues that hit them where they live, or in their purse or their wallet. They get engaged about immigration, their children's welfare, education. Or pets, if the number of cat, dog, three-toed sloth and hamster-bottom Internet memes are anything to go by. Plop a purring cat or a lapdog on every bench in the House of Commons and the viewing figures would shoot up. Only kidding . . .

3

The Nick Ferrari Political Plan

Seeing as the nation tunes in to my show over their Weetabix every weekday morning and there's nothing I enjoy more for breakfast than a lightly grilled politician, I might as well use my position to help give the public a voice, and find a way to re-engage them with politics.

For too long, we have witnessed privileged political professionals, unhelpfully trained in managing the media, screw up the issues that matter, even to the extent that many voters have stopped turning up to the polling stations altogether.

This is a travesty of representation. Times are hard and we could all do with strong leaders who identify with the pressures that ordinary individuals face every day.

We, the public, have incredibly sensitive nonsense detectors: telling the truth is the only way to calm our twitching antennae. It doesn't take special analytical skills or political knowledge to see through the cynical posturing that passes for real concern these days.

Please can we agree that nobody feels better for singing 'Baa, baa, green sheep' and return to calling 'personal access units' manholes?

Legislators really need to butt out of our personal lives. If they could just stop hectoring us for a minute and making everything either illegal or compulsory, the population can self-select those fit for breeding and we might even remember our own moral radar for 'doing the right thing'.

I have a vision that politicians can get back in touch with normality. In the post-Leveson-inquiry era, it is crucial to sidestep the PR intermediaries that create paranoid puppets spouting nothing but alliterative headlines. We should all be allowed to initiate embarrassingly frank discussions that will not only generate entertainment, but also jolt everyone awake and help us to decide who deserves our vote.

None of the Above

In the meantime, as a way of being able to register your vote while also saying you have absolutely no faith in politicians, there should be a None of the Above Party.

We would stand for caring about all the ways in which our country is run, but we would be making a firm stand for a different kind of politics.

We can't identify with most of our politicians. That's why the Nick Ferrari blueprint is anti-politics by anti-politicians.

Did you know there's a law against registering as 'none of the above' and running for election? A couple of people have changed their name by deed poll to None-of-the-Above. You've got to love human ingenuity. One bloke in Essex, because he was named None-of-the-Above, was listed as Above, None-of-the, and came at the top of the list. But then there's also a NOTA Party, which actually exists.

So the first thing we need to do is to get the

law changed, so that we can be the None of the Above Party.

I would usher in a new breed of leaders who have earned their stripes in a relevant field, who are able to cut through the pretence, and who do not pretend to inhuman infallibility. For instance, my foreign secretary would be Prince Philip. Undoubtedly. Well travelled, well connected and unhindered by the conventional rules of diplomacy, come to think of it, he's born to the role.

We don't want hordes of Oxbridge twerps running the country; we need to widen our nets. I think it's good that in America you can be a fairly average B-movie actor and then the next thing you know, you're in the White House and you're the president. America's culture celebrates the individual, so that in the US you literally can go from the outhouse to the White House. We're still far too class-ridden here in the UK.

Arnold Schwarzenegger turned into a particularly bulky governor for California. Well, he can come over here and I will give him International Development, because then each time he leaves Bangladesh, he will be heard to say, 'Ahl be baaak.'

The UK will regain the sense of humour that made our comedies such successful exports, and our leaders will stop taking themselves so seriously.

We'll be like the Tea Party, but funnier

Both the problem and the joy of UKIP is that it's the cat among the proverbials. UKIP's a one-trick pony, that's all. So we need to take what they did, running through the British establishment like a dose of Epsom salts, but put it together with some real grown-up policies and appoint a fleet of truth-telling politicians who know their stuff.

I'm a small-A anarchist — not like Russell Brand, who seems to want to throw the baby out with the bathwater, but I do like throwing the whole system up in the air and seeing where it lands.

I feel sorry for Farage in a way, because he attracted a minority with extreme and eccentric views, but then it is a relatively new party. I'm sure, as and when we launch the None of the Above Party, I'm going to attract some nutters, because we're seeking to do something outside the norm. That's the whole point. Normal people won't want to come and join, but I don't want people who would feel comfortable in the normal Conservative Party, or the Lib Dems, or Labour.

Having said that, there would have to be very careful and non-stop vetting. Our politicians need to pass the pub test to prove they can act normally in a social situation and all our members would have to take me for an evening out, for dinner at a particularly fine restaurant, where we would go through the details of their romantic and financial background.

Once he or she had satisfied me that they were a 'good egg', or a good lass, they're in.

They need to be decent, hard-working citizens but, other than that, the more eccentric the better. I want to be able to enjoy dinner in vibrant company, I don't want to grit my teeth and suppress my yawns. We will instantly reject anyone who conforms to the three political party stereotypes.

When you watch the elections, you've got these terribly serious, intoned voices saying, 'Well, now we go to the key count at Sunderland East,' and then you see this shining, scrubbed Conservative face; you see the Labour guy in a jacket with leather patches on the elbows (he's always looking angry — I went for summer drinks with the Labour Party the other day, they're all getting free wine and biscuits, but they still look angry. What are they angry about?); you see the Lib Dem in sandals, and various others. 'I am the returning officer and I hereby give the result . . .' And then you see a guy dressed as a pantomime horse!

Now that's what I call politics. The UK populace is a right motley crew and yet our main representatives are terribly boring. It's time for a new Screaming Lord Sutch. That would introduce a bit of colour to the proceedings, and provide a little light relief from all the hand-wringing. The Monster Raving Loony Party are still running and they've had council seats in various different places: people have voted them in, again and again and again; they've been shocked by their own electoral success. I'm only surprised we haven't had a Monster Raving Loony prime minister. What's that you say?

I mean, the Mayor of Hartlepool campaigned and won three times *dressed as a monkey*. The idea comes from their local folklore about the Napoleonic War: apparently there was a French shipwreck and its sole survivor, who happened to be a monkey, washed up wearing a French uniform. An impromptu trial was held and the Hartlepudlians hanged the monkey for not answering any questions — they thought he might be a spy. There's a special song they sing about this monkey, especially at the football.

Well, the Hartlepool monkey's definitely in my party. He'll get the Agriculture and Fisheries Ministry.

There are going to be some changes around here

If you happen to be a woman, promise me this: if your husband becomes leader of a political party, at the end of the party political conference, please assure me that you won't go racing up to your husband to hug and kiss him and wave out to the party faithful at the end of his speech.

Is there anything more demeaning to a wife than the fact that she has to sit there in the front row, eyes glistening with tears of admiration, love and support, for the husband who she very possibly despises — when they've had a bloody great row that morning about the fact that he hasn't seen the children for three weeks because he's been writing a boring speech, and he's been locked away with all his advisers for days on end and the marriage is on the point of breakdown — but she has to look at him like their eyes have just met across the student bar?

I give you this promise: no woman in my life, or indeed man if I decide to change, would ever have to come and hug me at the end of my speech. It would be the exact opposite. The press and party colleagues would go to her afterwards and she'd say, 'Well, that was a load of drivel, wasn't it? He speaks a load of rubbish — I don't believe a word he says! He said he'd put the shelves up in the bathroom last Thursday, and they've still not gone up.' That's one thing I truly loathe, and it wouldn't happen in my party.

There will be no room for fakes. All politicians will have to attend a school that will be run rather like a sports academy. There will be a compulsory curriculum and the headmaster will be the coach of the German World Cup football team, the one with the strange hair who is clearly an absolute master tactician and a merciless disciplinarian. Those kids weren't allowed in to go and have a shower until they'd nailed ten penalties in a row. You just knew in the World Cup that if you faced Germany at penalties there was absolutely no point.

Much as we have finishing schools and military academies such as Sandhurst, we are going to develop a finishing school for politicians run along those lines. Lessons will include speaking normally and dressing so that you don't look like a failed estate agent or mobile-phone salesman.

Politicians will learn how to kiss a baby without looking repugnant, how to make a good and genuine apology, how to be offensive to Europeans in six different languages, and how to prune their wisteria because, remember, we had to pay for that to be done on the houses of quite a few of the MPs, including David Cameron's. If MPs can be taught how to tend to their own gardens, including building a duck house, taxpayers could save a lot of money.

We would bring the humanity back into politics and this hideous 'computer-says-no' mentality and the robotic programming of politicians would all be things of the past.

Each of my cabinet would have a day, or part of a day, set aside — so Monday might be health, Tuesday might be education, Wednesday would be for the chancellor of the exchequer — where they just apologise.

People would be able to ring up and say, 'I just got my bloody tax bill and it's ridiculous! £17,000? It means I can't change the car.' And the chancellor would perhaps say: 'I'm very sorry about that but, honestly, if we don't collect your tax bill we can't treat Dora Wilkins in Croydon who desperately needs a hip operation on the NHS.' Someone would call to say, 'My son did very badly in his GCSEs.' And the Minister for Education could just say, 'I'm very sorry about that.' Everybody gets things wrong. Saying sorry is so powerful. Why don't people just do it?

There would be regular phone-ins, so that you can get directly through to high-office people in person and really shout at the people who run the country. How about that? Access-all-areas — the Nick Ferrari plan.

Now, about those grown-up policies . . .

The economy

Because Britain loves animals and they can calm you down, I think you should get tax rebates for the amount of time you spend with a pet. Preferably everyone will have their own pet, because that will make it easier for the taxman or woman.

If you can't have your own pet because you live in a block of flats, you should borrow other people's pets — ask them first. If you can prove that you've taken Rover for a nice walk around the heath, or that you've brushed Tiddles, wormed her and provided her morning milk and biccies then, a bit like the Australians have an immigration points system for access to the country, you will reap the tax benefits on your Pets Points Loyalty Card.

If I'm exhausted or hungover, I sometimes grab hold of my aged cat and sit there stroking her while I watch the opening titles of the morning news, before I get in the car. It is scientifically proven that it calms you down: it lowers your blood pressure. Some people can get away with a hamster, but everybody must have access to a pet or their taxes will increase. Give the public what they want and they will feel happier for it. And Britain is obsessed with animals.

As far as I'm concerned, though, the tax system in this country needs to be simplified. I don't blame the Arctic Monkeys and George Michael and Jimmy Carr. Don't blame them at all. Not for a second. They earn extraordinary amounts of money and it's totally understandable that they want to make everything, legally, as tax efficient as it can be. Now, you can argue and debate the morals of it, but that is the reality. The same with companies, whether it's a company selling mobile phones or providing coffee in the morning or whatever it might be — allegedly they're ripping us all off. Well, this isn't the companies' fault; this is the fault of those who legislate.

Apparently the tax code is so complicated, with so many bits of paper, that it would fill an average living room. Well, if you give someone all of that to deal with, they're going to find a loophole.

It's ridiculous. I sit with my accountant, who is a brilliant bloke, but he might as well be speaking to me in Sanskrit, I've absolutely no idea what he's saying.

I would say: right, if you earn above £80,000 a year then you will be taxed at 38 per cent. Done. If you run your own company, pencils are allowable, and lunch is 15 per cent, but holiday with the children to Greece, two weeks with car hire? No. Done. Let's keep things simple, people.

For my chancellor of the exchequer — until my corner shop employee turns up for the job — I'd have to go for Dame Vivienne Westwood. This extraordinary woman can sometimes look like a bag woman on a bad hair day who's been dragged through a hedge backwards, forwards and side-ways and then stood in the longest, hardest, roughest gale at the end of the pier for an eter-nity. Yet, people still clamour to buy anything that comes out with her name on out. Anyone who can make a fortune year in year out since the Boer War by flogging fashion that resembles the curtains from my maiden aunt's bedroom has got to be cute with cash.

Education

I think that, every now and again, without warning, pupils should be allowed to test their teachers on contemporary matters. So it would be perfectly acceptable that a teacher is suddenly asked, 'Who's your favourite Kardashian sister, Kim or Kourtney, Sir?'

If they're communicating with children who are obsessed with the Kardashians, then Mr Greaves the geography teacher needs to know who they are. So the children will occasionally ask them questions and if they fail three in a row, it's a full Ofsted inspection.

Now, you can agree or disagree, but at a stroke I'd bring back grammar schools. They were the single greatest tool of social mobility that this country's ever had, and it's tragic that David Cameron has turned his back on them.

The reason that they became so unpopular is: what do you do with the kids who aren't academic at age eleven? We don't have any problem with Johnny Boffin or Sarah Boffin, because they sailed through their eleven-plus and they're now at St Swithin's Grammar, and they're off. But the comprehensive system was, in some cases, seen to have failed — the kids were seen to be second-rate, which was simply not the case.

We have to accept that some children, try as hard as you like with the best teachers in the world, just won't be excited by algebra, you won't get them to read Shakespeare and they couldn't give a stuff about Chaucer. Let's be honest, and let's stop trying to force them into it. But they might be absolutely brilliant carpenters; they might be superb hairdressers.

Let's not have this terrible them and us distinction. Let's just embrace the fact that we're always going to have kids in every generation who are going be very happy to learn to be plumbers — and, my God, we need them — and let them start earning money as soon as they leave school rather than festering on their parents' sofas as 'NEETS' — people 'not in employment, education or training'.

We have to pay teachers more money, and really value them. And we need continuity. It saddens me that, along with health-care, the thing that every incoming government thinks it has to change is education. They all think they've got better ideas than those who went before. But children are our future, and yes, I know it's a cliché, but it's true.

Oh, and I'd make Jeremy Paxman the secretary of state for Education. Paxman gets the job because he knows all the answers from *University Challenge* and I can't even understand the questions, let alone get the answers.

Health-care

No politician ever gets up to say, 'We're no longer going to deliver all NHS health-care free at the point of use.' But I would. I absolutely would.

When I have my first heart attack because I'm so overweight, the NHS should be there for me, without question. Then they should say, 'Now, Mr Ferrari, we have saved your life, but we do expect you to show that you can lose some weight, because otherwise you're going to have another heart attack within the next couple of years. And if you do, and you haven't been seen to try to lose weight, you're not going to have free treatment. So off you go and try to lose a stone over the next eight months, and we'll encourage you.'

We're not just going to shout at you, 'Get off the scales, fatty! Try the salad bar, lard arse!' We will honestly do our best to try to assist you. If, however, you have another heart attack and you have clearly ignored the advice we gave — in fact, you've gained another chin and your ankles have given way — you will have to donate 10 to 15 per cent of the costs to save your life a second time.

Why, oh why, are we spending all this money on people who won't help themselves? Everyone needs to take individual responsibility and, if you don't, we're not going to pay for you. Government should help those who help themselves, so that we can afford to look after those who *really* can't.

Quite frankly, the NHS can't carry on as it is.

Just a few months before writing this book, I lost my mum. She reached ninety-three, which was a fantastic age, and I'm delighted and grateful for everything that the clinicians did. In reality, during the last few weeks of her life, I had to ask myself if it was actually a very pleasant experience for her to depart the world in that state. I wonder; I don't know. Unfortunately, she's not here to ask.

But someone somewhere has to make some tough decisions about this because we're all living longer. So for those of us who are being taxed, the demand on us to pay for those who are elderly or have health issues is just going to keep getting higher; we're going to pay ever higher taxes, just to stay where we are.

My health secretary is Bruce Forsyth. At his age, hosting *Strictly* right up until the last series, well, to do that at eighty-six is phenomenal. Apparently he's very good at yoga. That's his secret. Brucie can show us all how to cross our varicose-vein-ridden legs and balance on our liver-spotted heads and it will keep us out of the nursing homes until absolutely necessary.

Transport

What the hell are we doing, building HS2? Have you met a businessman or woman who wants to go to Sheffield ten minutes more quickly? Have you? I've not met one who's said, 'Oh, Nick, do you know what, my life would be transformed if I could get to Birmingham New Street eight minutes earlier.' All they're going to do is have another coffee! That's all that's going to happen. So no end of big coffee chains are wetting themselves with glee at the gallons of extra soya lattes and flat whites they're going to sell. That £50 billion could be so much better spent.

Politicians seem to be determined to get us all on bicycles and take us back to living like they do in Vietnam, which people seem to think is a marvellously simple and romantic way to travel, but I'd like to do it the other way. I think the £50 billion budgeted for HS2 should be spent on cable cars.

I used to take the children to Chessington where the best ride was the Skyride, a kind of monorail. You went around on a track above all of the animals and all of the rides and the water, and you had a great perspective and it felt lovely and relaxing.

That's what we need. I'll build a series of cable cars, running down most streets of the land that bring you into a central hub. What a glorious way to get to work. So you just walk out as you knot your tie and kiss your partner, 'Bye, bye, darling,' and then the cable car comes with gentle music playing, to transport you peacefully into the air.

It would be lovely. Think of the employment, people would be putting up cables all day long. It could be called the Vince Cable Car System.

The elderly could work as cable car guides, because they've lived in their areas all their lives. As you go around they could point things out: 'Do you know, that's where I went to school and before the bombs came in 1944, there was a lovely bakers . . .' You can wear noise-cancelling headphones if you'd rather block them out — they won't realise as they'll be staring out and imagining all the old sights. They might get a tip: 'Here's sixpence for your trouble.'

Sir Ranulph Fiennes is my transport secretary. He can get to the South Pole and back on a couple of old tennis rackets strapped to his feet, it's phenomenal. So he's definitely got Transport.

Defence

With the None of the Above Party, the country will never go to war unless the prime minister or one of his children is actually willing to put in a fair stint of military service. It's only fair. Even if they end up doing the cooking or driving, at least they will get an idea of what's actually going on out there — and how hard it can be for the army on limited resources.

I have huge respect for the military, and I think we're blessed with some fantastic men and women who serve in the armed forces. What disappoints me is that every six months the story comes around that a former leader of the army or chief of the general staff or Royal Navy admiral or captain of the sea has come forth and announced, 'We are perilously close — we cannot continue like this. Any more cuts and we wouldn't be able to defend ourselves against Zimbabwe; the Isle of Wight will be immediately annexed.'

It's ridiculous that the British army, which was once one of the most respected armies in the entire world has, in some areas, been reduced to resembling the Boy Scouts, because they've consistently had cut after cut after cut.

With the exception of General Lord Dannatt, this is very seldom said by anybody in a position of power, because they're under political pressure, and because that's what they're trained to do. When you're in the army, if you're cut off behind enemy lines, surrounded on all sides by soldiers brandishing Taser guns, and it seems as if you've got absolutely no chance, however difficult the situation is, you put together a plan because you're going to fight to the last man or woman to get out. But because they're trained to fight their way out of any hole, they make the best use of what they've got.

What they should say when they're handed these ridiculous budgets to work with is: 'I don't accept it. I'm not going to work. You're destroying the army.'

We need a military that challenges the government when it makes cuts — because this affects all of us.

Perhaps we all need a good war to sort us out. We can huddle round in the air-raid shelters and sing Vera Lynn songs. My defence secretary is Dame Vera Lynn. She's got us through some very hard times before and we can all trust her to do so again.

Home Affairs

With a name like Ferrari, it's no secret that I'm only a second-generation immigrant myself. It's not racist to want to keep the country together, including for those who, quite rightly, want to come here, work hard and build better lives for their families. But we have a duty: we owe it to ourselves and our children to keep the country functioning well.

Immigration was the topic that the traditional political class didn't want us — and that's me, but also my listeners — to talk about. Indeed, when William Hague was leader of the Conservative Party and they fought the general election in 2001, he actually agreed that they wouldn't debate immigration because it would be seen as racist, and he'd been in trouble before by saying that Britain was becoming a 'foreign land'.

What a terrible mis-step. It is not racist to want to ensure that your children have places in schools, that your children are able to get housing, that there are going to be enough jobs for them.

There was a Labour speechwriter called Andrew Neather who accidentally revealed in 2000 that early drafts of a speech he had written to argue for an increased foreign labour market originally stated that they wanted 'to rub the Right's nose in diversity' and create a multicultural society to 'render their arguments out of date'. To throw open the borders, as the Labour Party did, in order to 'rub the Right's nose in it'? That was criminal.

Race has taken off as such a massive issue because it is perceived, I would say probably rightly, others would say wrongly, that the public have not been able to have their say for years.

People have seen their schools become filled with children who cannot speak English and housing lists swell and they're sick of it. Admittedly, our hospitals wouldn't run without immigrants, but if you go to A&E because you've fallen off a ladder, you sit there thinking,

'Wow! This is just like waiting in Heathrow Terminal 5.'

Unfortunately, at the moment, terrorism and race are driving a lot of calls to my show, especially now that LBC has gone national. If you live in Blackburn or Birmingham or Leicester, you've possibly not had the opportunity to talk candidly about how you feel about your town if you happen to be white. On the BBC, the minute the presenter heard them say, 'Well, in all honesty I don't recognise Leicester any more. I think the whole town . . .' they would probably say, 'OH MY GOD!' Fade them out and they're gone.

I would always say, 'Look, as long as you explain to me what the problem is . . .' to which of course they respond, 'Well, they've all got different skin colour . . .' and I then point out that skin colour doesn't matter at all, and if they think they can keep their back door unlocked because only white people are walking past the back garden, they've got another thing coming.

However, in all my years of talking to ordinary folk on my show, I have found that what people hate is unfairness. They loathe it. Because, essentially, Britain is a pretty fair country, by and large. Sometimes we get things wrong, but generally we try to do things right.

There's one case in particular that struck me in recent years. It's the phenomenal story of a ninety-five-year-old woman living in Norfolk. She's been living in this village called Watton since she was born in 1919. Now, this particular part of the county is attracting a lot of new immigrants, I imagine to pick spuds and flowers and I don't know what else. I think that's great — these are the people who fuel the economy.

But doctors' surgeries are having to take people off their lists to accommodate the influx, and they're moving people around as their catchment areas are shrinking. This elderly woman, who's been in the same village and going to the same surgery all her life, was told she'd have to change to a new GP, in a town she rarely visits, in her nineties.

Apparently this decision cannot be reviewed, because looking at an individual case would be seen to be discriminatory. Where is the common sense in all of that? I fully believe that none of the newcomers or anyone living in her area would complain — they'd probably be the first to sign the petition to keep her. These are common values that all reasonable people hold.

The whole thing lacks fairness, and that's what makes my callers angry.

All that would stop under my government. Old women can choose their doctor. In fact, the doctor will make house calls.

Now, the thing that's wrong with the judicial system is quite straightforward: the punishments are often wholly disproportionate to the crimes. There's the classic example of the man who happened to be an illegal asylum seeker, who knocked down and killed a little girl and then drove off; when they eventually got him he was given eighteen months. Now eighteen months actually means nine months, unless you try to break out or burn down the prison. This has to change.

My party would say, 'You've got five years,' and you really do get five years. If you try to burn the prison, we'll double it. Mess about and we'll add to your term.

Once inside, they will be kept in jails with a flickering light bulb and no windows. The jails will all be in the north of Scotland, where the midges are. They will only be served porridge. This nonsense about ensuring there are vegetarian options will end. There won't be any more apologising because the dessert option wasn't very good that day.

What are we apologising to prisoners for? I don't mean we should actually brutalise the inmates, but they're in there because they've decided not to live by the laws of the land and we should not be obliged to provide them with an extensive menu or an up-to-date DVD library.

Kirstie Allsopp will be my home secretary. She won't let us get away with being soft — we'll all have to mind our ps and qs and stop being such wusses — but she will make sure that everything's tidy and organised and that our towns are full of well-maintained hanging baskets.

4

Is it time to be more French?

So, the time has come to ask . . . if a country gets the politicians it deserves, what on earth have we done to get this lot?

Well, when a nation disengages to the extent that the British electorate has, it's inevitable. You might say it's chicken and egg — if we had better politicians, we'd engage a lot more. But that's not good enough. If the people demand it, the politicians will change.

For starters, we should all be voting. It's our right to vote. I don't advocate legislation that forces people to vote. But, if there's no one worth voting for, we need to take it upon ourselves to be more vocal.

Over here, we have the idea that we need 100,000 people to sign a petition before it can eventually be debated in the House of Commons. We need to get a touch of the French about us. Shake things up. They held a nine-day rail strike in 2014. Nine days! When they hold a strike in France, they really hold a strike — they barricade the streets, they set fire to things, they behead the monarchy . . . Now, we don't want to go that far, but it would be the most extraordinary wake-up call if people suddenly became that impassioned. It would wake up the politicians and it might wake up the rest of us, too.

Where you have to admire the French is that, at the worst, perhaps a couple of lorry drivers are going to lose their spare tyres — I don't mean the ones around their waists, I mean the protestors will steal a few tyres because they burn so well — and some people are going to be late for their lunch, so sales of red wine in some pretty little village will slump a bit, or, in the worst-case scenario, you might miss a ferry.

Here, we get our targets all mixed up. The London riots went a bit national, at least two people lost their lives and businesses that families had built up for generations and private homes were burned. We shouldn't be destroying anything — we're seeking constructive dialogue. Sometimes peaceful protests can be great, but in the case of Occupy — the hippies who smoked dope outside St Paul's — they'd be better off going and learning about banking and reforming it from within, rather than spending weeks camped out, knitting rainbow-striped bobble hats and not working. I'd have got down with a microphone and said, 'You've got an hour, right? Clear off or we are coming in with the cavalry.'

These kinds of protestors are against everything: they're against bankers, capitalism, fracking, you name it, and they're a rather smelly bunch who travel around in the back of Ford Transits trying to find a cause. If you actually sat down with any of them and asked, 'What do you think this is going to achieve? How will sleeping outside St Paul's, preventing the schools from attending their church services this Christmas, help reform the banking industry?' they cannot offer an answer.

There's always the classic option, too: providing the politician doesn't get hurt it is quite funny to see Peter Mandelson with green ink all over his head, or Prescott immediately react with a punch when he was egged. It was impressive; he was quick. When the media got Blair to comment, he said, 'John is John.' What used to go on in Cabinet then? Because there was no love lost between him and Brown. Massive great fights! It must have been like Godzilla. 'Yeah. That's just John being John.'

In the end, though, what we have learned is that we're all going to have to up our game. We're all going to have to send the message that inane, vacuous, dull politicians coming out with statements that actually mean nothing will no longer be accepted.

We demand attention, and if we have to march with home-made placards or throw a few things around to remind you that we exist, so be it. Politicians need to see that the public is not going to lie down and stop voting just because they're so completely out of touch, incomprehensible and robotic. It's everybody's responsibility to pipe up.

We will not stand in our queues and mumble under our breath about political ineffectiveness and privilege. We will no longer pretend that we're taken in by PR-managed political stunts.

At the moment, when a politician tries to kiss your baby, it's a shallow attempt to curry favour. As we've seen, that's exactly what's wrong with politics in the UK. That politician might as well bite your baby and be done with it. That would be a more honest reflection of their interests.

But now that we're all heading into the new politics Nick Ferrari-style, sneaky baby-kissing hypocrites will have nowhere to hide. They will be far too busy listening to the more mature specimens of the human race, the ones that have fully developed vocal cords and reasoning skills. Politicians will engage with the humans that can vote for them, rather than ingratiating themselves with their babies in order to avoid difficult questions. Those days will be a thing of the past.

Pointing and laughing because the politicians are so hopelessly unengaged with the public will be entirely unnecessary when the Nick Ferrari political plan kicks in.

You might be laughing, but that will

be because the main candidate is dressed like a monkey and seems to be repeatedly apologising.

You'll be laughing for all the right reasons.

About LBC

LBC is Britain's only national news talk radio station. It tackles the big issues of the day, with intelligent, informed and provocative opinion from guests, listeners and presenters, including Nick Ferrari, James O'Brien, Shelagh Fogarty, Iain Dale, Ken Livingstone, David Mellor and Beverley Turner. LBC reaches 1.2 million people in Britain and is available on DAB digital radio, online at lbc.co.uk, through mobile apps, Sky Digital Channel 0112, Virgin Media Channel 919 and on 97.3FM in London.

About the Series

In this major new series, popular LBC presenters tackle the big issues in politics, current affairs and society. We might applaud their views; we might be outraged. But these short, sharp polemics are destined to generate controversy, discussion and debate — and lead Britain's conversation.

Titles in the series